The Motorcycle Queen of Miami

A Story Based on the Life of Bessie B. Stringfield

by Phyllis Lamattina

DEDICATION:

This book is dedicated to every woman who has decided to ride their own. Cheers! And to everyone who, despite obstacles in their life, did not give up nor conform to society's standards and lives life by their own rules. To you I say "Bravo!"

-Phyllis Lamattina
NYC 2015

The noisy banquet hall in Sturgis, South Dakota is standing room only for the 2002 Motorcycle Hall of Fame Luncheon honoring the years' inductees. Photographers and journalists from local and national publications are snapping pictures and interviewing biker celebrities as well as inductees who are present. Motorcyclists from the general public are also in attendance despite the gloomy weather and are in awe of the greatness surrounding them. The women attendees are especially interested in hearing about their predecessors who were triumphant over their obstacles. Each one of these honorees is a pioneer in the formerly male dominated sport/hobby. The emcee steps up to the podium and begins to speak about the posthumous inductee, Bessie Stringfield, who passed away in 1993.

As they begin to tell Bessie's story, they take us back to Jamaica circa 1911 where a baby is born in Kingston to a white woman and black father. The father exclaims, "This is a special girl!" as he holds his new daughter. Unfortunately, the joy is short lived as the following five years bring several challenges to their family. They experienced years of financial difficulties due to the lack of work available to Bessie's father. This then led to constant arguing and heavy drinking. With the frustration of not being able to provide for his family, Bessie's father became physically violent towards her mother. After a few years of this behavior, their neighbors could no longer keep their silence and called child services. Bessie was then brought to a local orphanage at the age of five.

A woman from Jamaican child services is holding Bessie in her arms at the entranceway to the Kingston Catholic Children's Home. She puts Bessie down and the orphanage administrator takes the hand of the inconsolable child and brings her inside.

Later that year in Boston, Massachusetts, a wealthy white couple is in a doctor's office and the wife is sobbing. Her husband is trying to console his wife as she has just found out that she is not able to bear children. The doctor's nurse enters the room with some literature exploring adoption. The woman wipes her tears and begins to read the documents. Her husband cradles her in his arms and she smiles. "It's going to be ok," he tells her. "We will adopt a child and have a family."

Bessie is brought to her new home in Boston. She is

awestruck as she walks into the home completely overwhelmed by her surroundings. Her adoptive mother takes her into her new room done up in frilly lace and the best of furniture. Her mother kneels down, holds the child's hand and tells her, "This is all yours Bessie. Welcome home."

    Bessie was an ideal child. She didn't give her mother any problems and always did what she was told. Sunday mass was a huge part of their life as the family was Irish Catholic and had very strong faith. Bessie's mother taught her to ask the Lord for what she wanted because He would give it to her.

    Right before her sixteenth birthday while they were having tea in the living room one Sunday after church, Bessie's mother asked her daughter what she wanted for her birthday. Both were dressed in their finest attire with white lace gloves and pillbox hats. Bessie thought about it for a bit while fidgeting with her linen napkin and then blurted out "I want a motorcycle!" Stunned, her mother kept her composure as she pursed her lips and said with a hint of annoyance in her voice, "Bessie, good girls don't ride motorcycles, it's not proper." Bessie said again, "I really, really want a motorcycle Momma."

Bessie's mother bought the motorcycle for her because it's what Bessie wanted. She mumbled under her breath, "Well you know Bessie, you are a good girl and never give me any trouble so I cannot say no to you! You are a feisty young lady, but a good daughter and deserve to have whatever you want in life." With this philosophy, Bessie was given anything that she desired from her parents.

Bessie's first bike was a blue 1928 Indian Scout. Bessie didn't know how to ride, but her mother always said, "Ask Our Lord Jesus Christ for what you need and He will listen" whenever she needed anything. And the "Man Upstairs," as she liked to call him, did indeed give her the skills to learn how to operate that motorcycle. She believed that He was always with her, especially when she rode her motorcycle.

At 19, Bessie wanted to ride her motorcycle everywhere. She bought her first Harley Davidson motorcycle that year. Much later in life she would declare after owning 27 of them, that Harley was "the only motorcycle ever made!" And they also had to be new and blue!

There were so many places to see in this great country but she didn't know where to go. Her deciding moment came when she was in her bedroom looking up at a map of the United States hanging on her wall. She tore it down enthusiastically and placed it on her bed. She ran to her purse, pulled out a penny and turned around with her back towards the bed. She threw the penny over her shoulder and said to herself, "wherever the penny lands, that's where I am riding to!" She did this each and every time she decided to go on a road trip! Over the years, she covered all 48 lower states.

Her first trip across the Deep South was especially overwhelming. Racism was a huge threat in the 1930's and good girls weren't exactly riding motorcycles across the country by themselves. She was riding on a road when she noticed a pickup truck of white men following her. She glanced in her mirror as they were getting close and trying to run her off the road. Bessie prayed to the Lord and asked for help. One of the men leaned out of the passenger side window and pointed a rifle at her. He yelled, "Hey you! Don't you know women aren't supposed to ride motorcycles?" He shot the gun up in the air, sat back in the truck and had a good chuckle with the other men thinking she will get flustered and fall; but Bessie's superior natural riding skills as well as her unwavering spirit allowed her to stay in control of the bike and she never lost her focus. She gripped the handlebars even tighter and continued to pray. This continued for the better part of thirty minutes and after several attempts of scaring her and shooting in the air, the men eventually turned off the road. They realized that this woman was not intimidated by them and it was a futile effort. Bessie then exhaled a sigh of relief and thanked the Lord for her safe escape from these men.

On another road trip she was once again in the south riding after a long rainy, windy day. She pulled into a filling station tired, hungry, sopping wet and in need of a warm, relaxing bath, but she needed fuel first. An older white gentleman came out to help her. She silently dreaded this encounter as she was thinking that it would be another racist man who didn't approve of her two wheeled travels. And, will most likely deny her gas as well as the use of the bathroom.

As the man approached her, he smiled. Bessie rubbed her eyes wondering if this was a hallucination! "How ya doing little lady?" he asked. Stunned by his southern hospitality, she replied, "I'm well sir. Very, very well!"

He invited her inside to take a break from the rain. He told her that the rain was just a passing storm and over the horizon it was clearing. They talked about motorcycles, her travels, her encounters with racism and the joy that motorcycling brought to her life. When the rain stopped, they went outside and she filled her tank with gas. When she reached for her wallet to pay him, he refused her money. He told her how much he admired her tenacity and said, "May God bless you in your travels." At that moment the sun peeked out thru the clouds and Bessie knew it was the Lord telling her that all would be fine. She drove off smiling and said a prayer for this man who became her Good Samaritan! Bessie had experienced kindness from fellow motorcyclists because of the camaraderie within the motorcycle community and from black families who took her in for the night on her road trips, but hardly ever from white folks. This man was one of many in her life who proved that kind, non-prejudiced people existed in the world. She then found a black family's home before nightfall and asked if she could stay there for the night. They welcomed Bessie with opened arms and chatted over dinner about her travels, eager to hear her adventures from the open road.

During World War II, Bessie became a United States Army civilian motorcycle dispatch rider. Her training was rigorous and she was the only woman in the unit along with six black men, but again that did not stop her. Her entire life was filled with obstacles which she met, challenged and overcame and this was no exception. Bessie was even more determined to succeed by performing these training maneuvers. She learned to make a bridge from tree limbs and rope so that she could cross swamps if a bridge was out. Her primary job as she traveled across the country was to carry documents from one military base to another. On her "61" blue Harley she proudly displayed the military crest on the front of the bike. She never did need to utilize the bridge-making skills.

As she traveled and was not allowed to stay in hotels, Bessie would create a makeshift pillow by rolling her jacket on the handlebars, stretch out and sleep on her bike in filling stations. Unless there was a willing black family to take her in, this was the only way she was able to rest. She always relied heavily on her strong faith to get her through these times. This happened every single time that she traveled, but Bessie was hardly discouraged by the inconvenience. She was riding her motorcycle, the place where she was most happy.

Bessie also performed in carnival stunt shows on her Indian motorcycle. Her positive, nothing-can-stop-me attitude paired with her natural skills as a rider earned her money to survive. She knew she could not live without riding. Bessie often wondered where this tenacity and love of motorcycling came from. She barely remembered her Jamaican parents and tried desperately to remember them, but never had a clear memory. So she eventually credited the only mother that she had ever known with cultivating her spirit for adventure and blind faith.

After the war and years as a stunt show rider, Bessie's home base in Boston became meaningless after her parents died. So in the late 1950's, she decided to move to the sunshine of Miami, Florida. It was in the Miami suburb of Opa Locka where she planted roots, bought a house and several years later became a licensed practical nurse. Bessie chose to live in the community of Bunche Park which was known for its population of black World War II veterans. However, the decision to settle in South Florida did not come without controversy. In Miami, the local police weren't as keen to see Bessie scoot around their city on two wheels. On several occasions, white police officers told her that "nigger women don't ride motorcycles."

   In true Bessie form, she refused to let these people stop her from doing what she loved most in life. So she continued to pray and ask the Lord to help these narrow minded people overcome their prejudices towards her. Bessie never lost faith in

God nor in the goodness of people regardless of the difficulties that she encountered over the years. Bessie's mother always reminded her about these types of people in the world and said to her, "Bessie don't pay them any mind. The Lord didn't give them the gift of compassion or the ability to be color blind."

In Miami there was one white police officer who took a liking to the feisty Bessie. Robert Jackson, or "Cap'n Jack" as Bessie liked to call him. He was with the Dade County Sheriff's Office. He guided and advised Bessie on what to do because many of her neighbors did not support her. Cap'n Jack was a kindhearted, good cop who despite seeing his share of criminal activity, still saw the good in humanity. And one thing he knew for sure, Bessie was a special young lady and his friend.

On many a hot summer night, Bessie and Cap'n Jack would sit on her front porch sharing stories mostly about her adventures on her motorcycle. One night Cap'n Jack said to Bessie, "BB, why don't you start your own motorcycle club?"
Bessie replied, "You know Cap'n Jack that's a great idea!" And the Iron Horse Motorcycle Club was born.

With the Iron Horse MC, Bessie ensured that all local motorcyclists were welcome. She knew first hand the emotional pain of prejudice and the exclusion of riders was not part of the fabric of the Iron Horse MC. She led many rides which benefitted the less fortunate in her community and helped foster the growing number of motorcyclists in the Miami area.

One hot Miami day, Bessie entered a flat track race to win some cash. She was fierce on the track and won the race. The organizer of the race greeted her when she hopped off the bike to claim her prize. When she removed her helmet to take a picture and wave to the cheering fans, the organizer pulled the money from her hand because she was a woman. He huffed away in disgust, but the other racers chuckled when they saw that they were outraced by a woman. Each of them were gracious and shook her hand. One man said to her, "What's your name? I want to remember it because someday I want to tell people that I shook your hand!" She replied, "My name is Bessie, and thank you." They shook hands and Bessie started her bike and left the grounds.

In between Bessie's eight solo cross-country motorcycle rides, she was married six times. In an interview, Bessie said her bikes had to be "new and blue, the only thing used were husbands!" She also told a reporter once, "During my day, if a woman kissed a man, they got married!" Her third husband, Arthur Stringfield said to Bessie during their divorce, "BB, can you do me one last favor?" Bessie nodded yes wondering what he was going to ask of her.

"BB, I need you to keep my last name, even if you marry again. I ask this of you because I know in my heart that one day you will make my name famous!"

Bessie replied, "Sure Arthur, I can do that."

Her dogs were her babies and she often let them ride with her on the bike since Bessie never had any children. Tragically, she lost three children with her first husband and never again pursued motherhood. She let the dogs lean their paws on the handlebars as she rode and exclaimed to reporters, "They think they are driving!" As Bessie's popularity in the Miami area increased mostly due to her antics on her motorcycle, local reporters took notice. Bessie would ride down the street standing on the seat of her Harley. The Miami reporters dubbed her "The Negro Motorcycle Queen of Miami" and later, "The Motorcycle Queen of Miami." Throughout all of her adventures and press attention in Miami, Cap'n Jack was there by her side supporting his friend.

Bessie led a fulfilled life in Miami. Her nursing career was rewarding and in her free time she traveled across the United States on her bike and led the Iron Horse MC. It wasn't until she was a bit older that her physician detected that she had an enlarged heart. He said that her heart was three times the size of a normal heart. A metaphor quite befitting for Bessie's incredible generosity. He tried to discourage her from riding during each visit, and they all ended with Bessie stating loudly, "Doc, if I don't ride I will die!" So she continued to ride.

As the emcee continues Bessie's story, the room in Sturgis is silent. Some audience members have tears in their eyes as they hold onto every word. The emcee continues Bessie's journey and speaks about her last years on earth.

The year was 1990, and the American Motorcycle Association honored Bessie at their inaugural exhibit at the Motorcycle Heritage Museum in Ohio. Bessie traveled to the museum and attended the ceremony. When asked by the press what she thought about the fuss over her, Bessie replied, "I was somethin'! What I did was fun and I loved it." She was also quite grateful to the Lord for blessing her with this accolade and for allowing her to do what she loved for so many decades.

Sadly in 1993, Bessie B. Stringfield succumbed to her heart condition and passed away at the age of 82. But she rode her Harley until the very end of her life just as she knew she would.

The emcee looked up at the crowd and continued, "And it is with great honor that I present to you, the 2002 Motorcycle Hall of Fame inductee, Bessie B. Stringfield. Thank you Bessie for paving the way for millions motorcycle enthusiasts. Especially women. We know you are watching over us and smiling and we are so very grateful to you." The crowd stood on its feet and gave Bessie B. Stringfield the proper ovation that was due to her. And at that very moment outside, the clouds started to part as a beam of sunlight lit up the Sturgis sky.

ACKNOWLEDGEMENTS:

Bessie's story has been inside of my head for eight years now. I was unsure of how I wanted it to be told until Fall 2014.

To my family especially to my dad & brother who first taught me to ride on a dirt bike as a teen and gave me the motorcycling bug!

To my cousin Denise Lamattina who has given me infinite support and guidance with this story.

To all my biker brothers & sisters with whom I have traveled thousands of miles with, especially those who taught me how to group ride- Anthony Miniaci, Kevin Bascome and the Islanders MC.

And to Anthony Miniaci, I also say thank you for being my in house editor as your words of wisdom and edits helped me tell Bessie's story the best way that I could!

To Karen Carlini, my dear friend and second editor who gave me the non-biker perspective and ability to write a story that will inspire everyone, not just bikers.

To my core four - Valerie Timmons, Palma Ingoglio, Cathy Bonelli and Alice Pollard whose friendship knows no bounds and have been through it all with me. God didn't bless me with sisters, but who needs a sister when you have friends that are family.

A sincere thank you to the amazing colleagues and bosses that I have had in the corporate world throughout the years. You are too many to mention, but you know who you are.

And finally, to the bosses and colleagues who verbally tortured me over these last few years, I save the biggest thanks for you. Because without darkness there is no light; and without hitting rock bottom, Bessie's story would never have been told.

-Phyllis Lamattina

NYC 2015

Made in the USA
San Bernardino,
CA